This journal belongs

to

_____

For more
inspirational content
follow us at:

 @healforgiveletgo

 @healforgiveletgo

Join our email list:

 healforgiveletgo@gmail.com

Please leave us a review on amazon.

I've got this!: A Daily Anxiety Check-In Journal for Women

Imprint: Independently published

Daily
PLANNER

Date _____

"By being yourself, you put something wonderful in the world that was not there before"
Edwin Elliot

WATER TRACKER
Fill in a drop for each glass you drink

ANXIETY CHECK
Rate your anxiety level (tick the circle)

◯ Not anxious

◯ A little anxious

◯ Somewhat anxious

◯ Pretty anxious

Thoughts

_____

_____

_____

_____

_____

_____

_____

Journal PROMPTS

❀ What three things make you the most anxious? ❀

❀ If I didn't experience anxiety, I wouldn't have learned this: ❀

What could you do right now that will make you really
❀ happy? ❀

Preparation TECHNIQUE

What's the situation?

What might make me feel anxious?

What can I say/ do to be prepared?

How have I handled it before?

Coping skills I can use

Grounding EXERCISE

🌸 Acknowledge 5 things you can touch 🌸

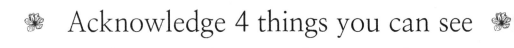

🌸 Acknowledge 4 things you can see 🌸

🌸 Name 3 things you are grateful for 🌸

🌸 Acknowledge 2 things you can hear 🌸

(Write it down in the circles)

Anxiety TRACKER

🌸 TRIGGER   REACTION 🌸

🌸 BETTER RESPONSE 🌸

🌸 HOW BAD WAS IT REALLY? 🌸

Color the squares (on a level of 1 to 5)

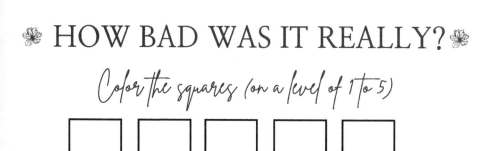

Daily PLANNER

Date _____

"The best way to find yourself is to lose yourself in the service of others"
Mahatma Gandhi

WATER TRACKER
Fill in a drop for each glass you drink

ANXIETY CHECK
Rate your anxiety level (tick the circle)

◯ Not anxious

◯ A little anxious

◯ Somewhat anxious

◯ Pretty anxious

Thoughts

_____

_____

_____

_____

_____

_____

_____

Journal PROMPTS

What three things make you the most anxious?

If I didn't experience anxiety, I wouldn't have learned this:

What could you do right now that will make you really happy?

Preparation TECHNIQUE

What's the situation?

What might make me feel anxious?

What can I say/ do to be prepared?

How have I handled it before?

Coping skills I can use

Grounding EXERCISE

❧ Acknowledge 5 things you can touch ❧

◯ ◯ ◯ ◯ ◯

❧ Acknowledge 4 things you can see ❧

◯ ◯ ◯ ◯

❧ Name 3 things you are grateful for ❧

◯ ◯ ◯

❧ Acknowledge 2 things you can hear ❧

◯ ◯

(Write it down in the circles)

Anxiety TRACKER

❀ TRIGGER

REACTION ❀

❀ BETTER RESPONSE ❀

❀ HOW BAD WAS IT REALLY? ❀

Color the squares (on a level of 1 to 5)

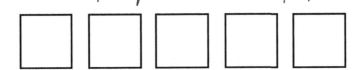

Daily PLANNER

Date _____

"Don't lose your real self in the search for acceptance by others"
Lora A.R.

WATER TRACKER
Fill in a drop for each glass you drink

ANXIETY CHECK
Rate your anxiety level (tick the circle)

○ Not anxious

○ A little anxious

○ Somewhat anxious

○ Pretty anxious

Thoughts

_____
_____
_____
_____
_____
_____
_____
_____

Journal PROMPTS

❀ What three things make you the most anxious? ❀

❀ If I didn't experience anxiety, I wouldn't have learned this: ❀

What could you do right now that will make you really
❀ happy? ❀

Preparation TECHNIQUE

What's the situation?

What might make me feel anxious?

What can I say/ do to be prepared?

How have I handled it before?

Coping skills I can use

Grounding EXERCISE

❀ Acknowledge 5 things you can touch ❀

( ) ( ) ( ) ( ) ( )

❀ Acknowledge 4 things you can see ❀

( ) ( ) ( ) ( )

❀ Name 3 things you are grateful for ❀

( ) ( ) ( )

❀ Acknowledge 2 things you can hear ❀

( ) ( )

(Write it down in the circles)

Anxiety TRACKER

❀ TRIGGER   REACTION ❀

❀ BETTER RESPONSE ❀

❀ HOW BAD WAS IT REALLY? ❀

Color the squares (on a level of 1 to 5)

☐ ☐ ☐ ☐ ☐

Daily
PLANNER

Date _____

"Happiness depends upon ourselves"
Aristotle

WATER TRACKER
Fill in a drop for each glass you drink

ANXIETY CHECK
Rate your anxiety level (tick the circle)

◯ Not anxious

◯ A little anxious

◯ Somewhat anxious

◯ Pretty anxious

Thoughts

_____

_____

_____

_____

_____

_____

_____

_____

Journal PROMPTS

❀ What three things make you the most anxious? ❀

❀ If I didn't experience anxiety, I wouldn't have learned this: ❀

What could you do right now that will make you really
❀ happy? ❀

Preparation TECHNIQUE

What's the situation?

What might make me feel anxious?

What can I say/ do to be prepared?

How have I handled it before?

Coping skills I can use

Grounding EXERCISE

🌸 Acknowledge 5 things you can touch 🌸

○ ○ ○ ○ ○

🌸 Acknowledge 4 things you can see 🌸

○ ○ ○ ○

🌸 Name 3 things you are grateful for 🌸

○ ○ ○

🌸 Acknowledge 2 things you can hear 🌸

○ ○

(Write it down in the circles)

Anxiety TRACKER

☘ TRIGGER   REACTION ☘

☘ BETTER RESPONSE ☘

☘ HOW BAD WAS IT REALLY? ☘

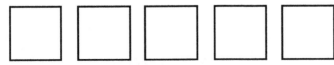

Color the squares (on a level of 1 to 5)

Daily PLANNER

Date _____

"You have to expect things of yourself before you can do them"
Michael Jordan

WATER TRACKER
Fill in a drop for each glass you drink

ANXIETY CHECK
Rate your anxiety level (tick the circle)

○ Not anxious

○ A little anxious

○ Somewhat anxious

○ Pretty anxious

Thoughts

_____

_____

_____

_____

_____

_____

_____

_____

Journal PROMPTS

❀ What three things make you the most anxious? ❀

❀ If I didn't experience anxiety, I wouldn't have learned this: ❀

What could you do right now that will make you really
❀ happy? ❀

Preparation TECHNIQUE

What's the situation?

What might make me feel anxious?

What can I say/ do to be prepared?

How have I handled it before?

Coping skills I can use

Grounding EXERCISE

Acknowledge 5 things you can touch

◯ ◯ ◯ ◯ ◯

Acknowledge 4 things you can see

◯ ◯ ◯ ◯

Name 3 things you are grateful for

◯ ◯ ◯

Acknowledge 2 things you can hear

◯ ◯

(Write it down in the circles)

Anxiety TRACKER

🌸 TRIGGER

REACTION 🌸

🌸 BETTER RESPONSE 🌸

🌸 HOW BAD WAS IT REALLY? 🌸

Color the squares (on a level of 1 to 5)

Daily PLANNER

Date _____

"They can because they think they can"
Virgil

WATER TRACKER
Fill in a drop for each glass you drink

ANXIETY CHECK
Rate your anxiety level (tick the circle)

◯ Not anxious

◯ A little anxious

◯ Somewhat anxious

◯ Pretty anxious

Thoughts

_____
_____
_____
_____
_____
_____
_____
_____

Journal PROMPTS

❀ What three things make you the most anxious? ❀

❀If I didn't experience anxiety, I wouldn't have learned this: ❀

What could you do right now that will make you really
❀ happy? ❀

Preparation TECHNIQUE

What's the situation?

What might make me feel anxious?

What can I say/ do to be prepared?

How have I handled it before?

Coping skills I can use

Grounding EXERCISE

🌸 Acknowledge 5 things you can touch 🌸

◯ ◯ ◯ ◯ ◯

🌸 Acknowledge 4 things you can see 🌸

◯ ◯ ◯ ◯

🌸 Name 3 things you are grateful for 🌸

◯ ◯ ◯

🌸 Acknowledge 2 things you can hear 🌸

◯ ◯

(Write it down in the circles)

Anxiety TRACKER

☙ TRIGGER ❧   REACTION ❧

☙ BETTER RESPONSE ❧

☙ HOW BAD WAS IT REALLY? ❧

Color the squares (on a level of 1 to 5)

☐ ☐ ☐ ☐ ☐

Daily PLANNER

Date _____

"There is no one giant step that does it. It's a lot of little steps"
Peter A. Cohen

WATER TRACKER
Fill in a drop for each glass you drink

ANXIETY CHECK
Rate your anxiety level (tick the circle)

○ Not anxious

○ A little anxious

○ Somewhat anxious

○ Pretty anxious

Thoughts

_____

_____

_____

_____

_____

_____

_____

_____

Journal PROMPTS

What three things make you the most anxious?

If I didn't experience anxiety, I wouldn't have learned this:

What could you do right now that will make you really happy?

Preparation TECHNIQUE

What's the situation?

What might make me feel anxious?

What can I say/ do to be prepared?

How have I handled it before?

Coping skills I can use

Grounding EXERCISE

Acknowledge 5 things you can touch

Acknowledge 4 things you can see

Name 3 things you are grateful for

Acknowledge 2 things you can hear

(Write it down in the circles)

Anxiety TRACKER

❀ TRIGGER   **REACTION ❀**

❀ BETTER RESPONSE ❀

❀ HOW BAD WAS IT REALLY? ❀

Color the squares (on a level of 1 to 5)

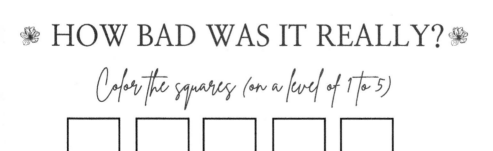

Daily PLANNER

Date _____

"It doesn't matter how slowly you go so long as you do not stop"
Confucius

WATER TRACKER
Fill in a drop for each glass you drink

(water drop illustrations)

ANXIETY CHECK
Rate your anxiety level (tick the circle)

○ Not anxious

○ A little anxious

○ Somewhat anxious

○ Pretty anxious

Thoughts

_____

_____

_____

_____

_____

_____

_____

Journal PROMPTS

What three things make you the most anxious?

If I didn't experience anxiety, I wouldn't have learned this:

What could you do right now that will make you really happy?

Preparation TECHNIQUE

What's the situation?

What might make me feel anxious?

What can I say/ do to be prepared?

How have I handled it before?

Coping skills I can use

Grounding EXERCISE

Acknowledge 5 things you can touch

◯ ◯ ◯ ◯ ◯

Acknowledge 4 things you can see

◯ ◯ ◯ ◯

Name 3 things you are grateful for

◯ ◯ ◯

Acknowledge 2 things you can hear

◯ ◯

(Write it down in the circles)

Anxiety TRACKER

❀ TRIGGER   REACTION ❀

❀ BETTER RESPONSE ❀

❀ HOW BAD WAS IT REALLY? ❀

Color the squares (on a level of 1 to 5)

Daily PLANNER

Date _____

"First understand and then act"
C. Jay

WATER TRACKER
Fill in a drop for each glass you drink

ANXIETY CHECK
Rate your anxiety level (tick the circle)

◯ Not anxious

◯ A little anxious

◯ Somewhat anxious

◯ Pretty anxious

Thoughts

_____
_____
_____
_____
_____
_____
_____
_____

Journal PROMPTS

What three things make you the most anxious?

If I didn't experience anxiety, I wouldn't have learned this:

What could you do right now that will make you really happy?

Preparation TECHNIQUE

What's the situation?

What might make me feel anxious?

What can I say/ do to be prepared?

How have I handled it before?

Coping skills I can use

Grounding EXERCISE

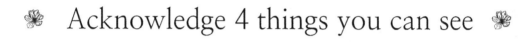 Acknowledge 5 things you can touch

○ ○ ○ ○ ○

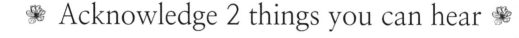 Acknowledge 4 things you can see

○ ○ ○ ○

Name 3 things you are grateful for

○ ○ ○

Acknowledge 2 things you can hear

○ ○

(Write it down in the circles)

Anxiety TRACKER

TRIGGER   REACTION

BETTER RESPONSE

HOW BAD WAS IT REALLY?

Color the squares (on a level of 1 to 5)

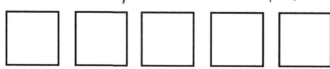

Daily PLANNER

Date _____

"Optimism is the foundation of courage"
Nicholas M. Butler

WATER TRACKER
Fill in a drop for each glass you drink

ANXIETY CHECK
Rate your anxiety level (tick the circle)

◯ Not anxious

◯ A little anxious

◯ Somewhat anxious

◯ Pretty anxious

Thoughts

_____
_____
_____
_____
_____
_____
_____

Journal PROMPTS

❁ What three things make you the most anxious? ❁

❁ If I didn't experience anxiety, I wouldn't have learned this: ❁

What could you do right now that will make you really
❁ happy? ❁

Preparation TECHNIQUE

What's the situation?

What might make me feel anxious?

What can I say/ do to be prepared?

How have I handled it before?

Coping skills I can use

Grounding EXERCISE

❀ Acknowledge 5 things you can touch ❀

◯ ◯ ◯ ◯ ◯

❀ Acknowledge 4 things you can see ❀

◯ ◯ ◯ ◯

❀ Name 3 things you are grateful for ❀

◯ ◯ ◯

❀ Acknowledge 2 things you can hear ❀

◯ ◯

(Write it down in the circles)

Anxiety TRACKER

❁ TRIGGER   REACTION ❁

❁ BETTER RESPONSE ❁

❁ HOW BAD WAS IT REALLY? ❁

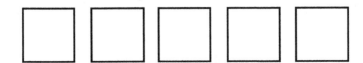

Color the squares (on a level of 1 to 5)

□ □ □ □ □

Daily PLANNER

Date _____

"You'll never find a rainbow if you're looking down"
Charlie Chaplin

WATER TRACKER
Fill in a drop for each glass you drink

ANXIETY CHECK
Rate your anxiety level (tick the circle)

◯ Not anxious

◯ A little anxious

◯ Somewhat anxious

◯ Pretty anxious

Thoughts

_____
_____
_____
_____
_____
_____
_____
_____

Journal PROMPTS

❀ What three things make you the most anxious? ❀

❀ If I didn't experience anxiety, I wouldn't have learned this: ❀

What could you do right now that will make you really
❀ happy? ❀

Preparation TECHNIQUE

What's the situation?

What might make me feel anxious?

What can I say/ do to be prepared?

How have I handled it before?

Coping skills I can use

Grounding EXERCISE

Acknowledge 5 things you can touch

○ ○ ○ ○ ○

Acknowledge 4 things you can see

○ ○ ○ ○

Name 3 things you are grateful for

○ ○ ○

Acknowledge 2 things you can hear

○ ○

(Write it down in the circles)

ANXIETY TRACKER

❀ TRIGGER

REACTION ❀

❀ BETTER RESPONSE ❀

❀ HOW BAD WAS IT REALLY? ❀

Color the squares (on a level of 1 to 5)

Daily PLANNER

Date _____

"Self Care is not selfish"
Madison Inouye

WATER TRACKER
Fill in a drop for each glass you drink

ANXIETY CHECK
Rate your anxiety level (tick the circle)

◯ Not anxious

◯ A little anxious

◯ Somewhat anxious

◯ Pretty anxious

Thoughts

_____
_____
_____
_____
_____
_____
_____

Journal
PROMPTS

🌸 What three things make you the most anxious? 🌸

🌸 If I didn't experience anxiety, I wouldn't have learned this: 🌸

What could you do right now that will make you really
🌸 happy? 🌸

Preparation TECHNIQUE

What's the situation?

What might make me feel anxious?

What can I say/ do to be prepared?

How have I handled it before?

Coping skills I can use

Grounding EXERCISE

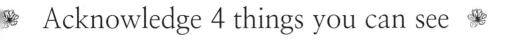

❀ Acknowledge 5 things you can touch ❀

○ ○ ○ ○ ○

❀ Acknowledge 4 things you can see ❀

○ ○ ○ ○

❀ Name 3 things you are grateful for ❀

○ ○ ○

❀ Acknowledge 2 things you can hear ❀

○ ○

(Write it down in the circles)

Anxiety TRACKER

❀ TRIGGER   REACTION ❀

❀ BETTER RESPONSE ❀

❀ HOW BAD WAS IT REALLY? ❀

Color the squares (on a level of 1 to 5)

☐ ☐ ☐ ☐ ☐

Daily PLANNER

Date _____

"Care is the best action"
Thirdman

WATER TRACKER
Fill in a drop for each glass you drink

ANXIETY CHECK
Rate your anxiety level (tick the circle)

◯ Not anxious

◯ A little anxious

◯ Somewhat anxious

◯ Pretty anxious

Thoughts

_____
_____
_____
_____
_____
_____
_____

Journal PROMPTS

❀ What three things make you the most anxious? ❀

❀If I didn't experience anxiety, I wouldn't have learned this:❀

What could you do right now that will make you really
❀ happy? ❀

Preparation TECHNIQUE

What's the situation?

What might make me feel anxious?

What can I say/ do to be prepared?

How have I handled it before?

Coping skills I can use

Grounding EXERCISE

❀ Acknowledge 5 things you can touch ❀

( ) ( ) ( ) ( ) ( )

❀ Acknowledge 4 things you can see ❀

( ) ( ) ( ) ( )

❀ Name 3 things you are grateful for ❀

( ) ( ) ( )

❀ Acknowledge 2 things you can hear ❀

( ) ( )

(Write it down in the circles)

Anxiety TRACKER

TRIGGER　　　　REACTION

BETTER RESPONSE

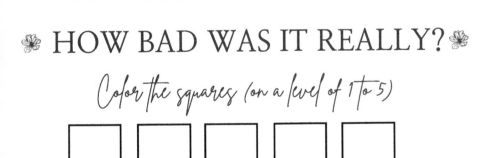

HOW BAD WAS IT REALLY?

Color the squares (on a level of 1 to 5)

☐ ☐ ☐ ☐ ☐

Daily PLANNER

Date _____

"Pessimism leads to weakness, optimism to power"
William James

WATER TRACKER
Fill in a drop for each glass you drink

ANXIETY CHECK
Rate your anxiety level (tick the circle)

◯ Not anxious

◯ A little anxious

◯ Somewhat anxious

◯ Pretty anxious

Thoughts

_____

_____

_____

_____

_____

_____

_____

_____

Journal PROMPTS

❀ What three things make you the most anxious? ❀

❀ If I didn't experience anxiety, I wouldn't have learned this: ❀

What could you do right now that will make you really ❀ happy? ❀

Preparation TECHNIQUE

What's the situation?

What might make me feel anxious?

What can I say/ do to be prepared?

How have I handled it before?

Coping skills I can use

Grounding EXERCISE

Acknowledge 5 things you can touch

◯ ◯ ◯ ◯ ◯

Acknowledge 4 things you can see

◯ ◯ ◯ ◯

Name 3 things you are grateful for

◯ ◯ ◯

Acknowledge 2 things you can hear

◯ ◯

(Write it down in the circles)

Anxiety TRACKER

❀ TRIGGER   REACTION ❀

❀ BETTER RESPONSE ❀

❀ HOW BAD WAS IT REALLY? ❀

Color the squares (on a level of 1 to 5)

Daily PLANNER

Date _____

"Worry is the interest paid by those who borrow trouble"
George Washington

WATER TRACKER
Fill in a drop for each glass you drink

◯ ◯ ◯ ◯ ◯
◯ ◯ ◯ ◯ ◯

ANXIETY CHECK
Rate your anxiety level (tick the circle)

◯ Not anxious

◯ A little anxious

◯ Somewhat anxious

◯ Pretty anxious

Thoughts

_____
_____
_____
_____
_____
_____
_____
_____

Journal PROMPTS

❀ What three things make you the most anxious? ❀

❀ If I didn't experience anxiety, I wouldn't have learned this: ❀

What could you do right now that will make you really
❀ happy? ❀

Preparation TECHNIQUE

What's the situation?

What might make me feel anxious?

What can I say/ do to be prepared?

How have I handled it before?

Coping skills I can use

Grounding EXERCISE

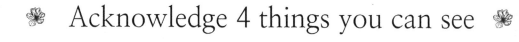
🌸 Acknowledge 5 things you can touch 🌸

◯ ◯ ◯ ◯ ◯

🌸 Acknowledge 4 things you can see 🌸

◯ ◯ ◯ ◯

🌸 Name 3 things you are grateful for 🌸

◯ ◯ ◯

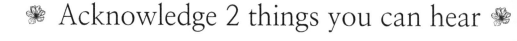
🌸 Acknowledge 2 things you can hear 🌸

◯ ◯

(Write it down in the circles)

Anxiety TRACKER

❀ TRIGGER   REACTION ❀

❀ BETTER RESPONSE ❀

❀ HOW BAD WAS IT REALLY? ❀

Color the squares (on a level of 1 to 5)

Daily PLANNER

Date _____

"Today is the tomorrow you worried about yesterday"
Dale Carnegie

WATER TRACKER
Fill in a drop for each glass you drink

ANXIETY CHECK
Rate your anxiety level (tick the circle)

◯ Not anxious

◯ A little anxious

◯ Somewhat anxious

◯ Pretty anxious

Thoughts

_____
_____
_____
_____
_____
_____
_____

Journal PROMPTS

❀ What three things make you the most anxious? ❀

❀ If I didn't experience anxiety, I wouldn't have learned this: ❀

What could you do right now that will make you really
❀ happy? ❀

Preparation TECHNIQUE

What's the situation?

What might make me feel anxious?

What can I say/ do to be prepared?

How have I handled it before?

Coping skills I can use

Grounding EXERCISE

🌸 Acknowledge 5 things you can touch 🌸

🌸 Acknowledge 4 things you can see 🌸

🌸 Name 3 things you are grateful for 🌸

🌸 Acknowledge 2 things you can hear 🌸

(Write it down in the circles)

Anxiety TRACKER

❀ TRIGGER   REACTION ❀

❀ BETTER RESPONSE ❀

❀ HOW BAD WAS IT REALLY? ❀

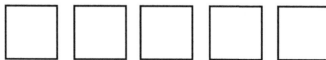

Color the squares (on a level of 1 to 5)

☐ ☐ ☐ ☐ ☐

Daily PLANNER

Date _____

"Silent gratitude isn't much use to anyone"
Gladys Bertha

WATER TRACKER
Fill in a drop for each glass you drink

💧 💧 💧 💧 💧

💧 💧 💧 💧 💧

ANXIETY CHECK
Rate your anxiety level (tick the circle)

○ Not anxious

○ A little anxious

○ Somewhat anxious

○ Pretty anxious

Thoughts

_____

_____

_____

_____

_____

_____

_____

_____

Journal PROMPTS

❀ What three things make you the most anxious? ❀

❀If I didn't experience anxiety, I wouldn't have learned this: ❀

What could you do right now that will make you really
❀ happy? ❀

Preparation TECHNIQUE

What's the situation?

What might make me feel anxious?

What can I say/ do to be prepared?

How have I handled it before?

Coping skills I can use

Grounding EXERCISE

🌸 Acknowledge 5 things you can touch 🌸

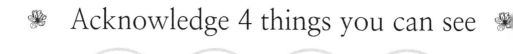

◯ ◯ ◯ ◯ ◯

🌸 Acknowledge 4 things you can see 🌸

◯ ◯ ◯ ◯

🌸 Name 3 things you are grateful for 🌸

◯ ◯ ◯

🌸 Acknowledge 2 things you can hear 🌸

◯ ◯

(Write it down in the circles)

Anxiety TRACKER

🌸 TRIGGER REACTION 🌸

🌸 BETTER RESPONSE 🌸

🌸 HOW BAD WAS IT REALLY? 🌸

Color the squares (on a level of 1 to 5)

☐ ☐ ☐ ☐ ☐

Daily PLANNER

Date _____

"Meditation is the tongue of the soul and the language of our spirit"
Jeremy Taylor

WATER TRACKER
Fill in a drop for each glass you drink

ANXIETY CHECK
Rate your anxiety level (tick the circle)

◯ Not anxious

◯ A little anxious

◯ Somewhat anxious

◯ Pretty anxious

Thoughts

_____
_____
_____
_____
_____
_____
_____

Journal PROMPTS

What three things make you the most anxious?

If I didn't experience anxiety, I wouldn't have learned this:

What could you do right now that will make you really happy?

Preparation TECHNIQUE

What's the situation?

What might make me feel anxious?

What can I say/ do to be prepared?

How have I handled it before?

Coping skills I can use

Grounding EXERCISE

❀ Acknowledge 5 things you can touch ❀

〇 〇 〇 〇 〇

❀ Acknowledge 4 things you can see ❀

〇 〇 〇 〇

❀ Name 3 things you are grateful for ❀

〇 〇 〇

❀ Acknowledge 2 things you can hear ❀

〇 〇

(Write it down in the circles)

Anxiety TRACKER

TRIGGER **REACTION**

BETTER RESPONSE

HOW BAD WAS IT REALLY?

Color the squares (on a level of 1 to 5)

☐ ☐ ☐ ☐ ☐

Daily PLANNER

Date _____

"Meditation is the soul's perspective glass"
Owen Feltham

WATER TRACKER
Fill in a drop for each glass you drink

ANXIETY CHECK
Rate your anxiety level (tick the circle)

- ◯ Not anxious
- ◯ A little anxious
- ◯ Somewhat anxious
- ◯ Pretty anxious

Thoughts

_____
_____
_____
_____
_____
_____
_____
_____

Journal PROMPTS

❀ What three things make you the most anxious? ❀

❀ If I didn't experience anxiety, I wouldn't have learned this: ❀

What could you do right now that will make you really
❀ happy? ❀

Preparation TECHNIQUE

What's the situation?

What might make me feel anxious?

What can I say/ do to be prepared?

How have I handled it before?

Coping skills I can use

Grounding EXERCISE

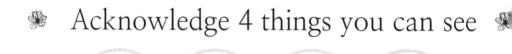
Acknowledge 5 things you can touch

○ ○ ○ ○ ○

Acknowledge 4 things you can see

○ ○ ○ ○

Name 3 things you are grateful for

○ ○ ○

Acknowledge 2 things you can hear

○ ○

(Write it down in the circles)

Anxiety TRACKER

❀ TRIGGER ❀ REACTION ❀

❀ BETTER RESPONSE ❀

❀ HOW BAD WAS IT REALLY? ❀

Color the squares (on a level of 1 to 5)

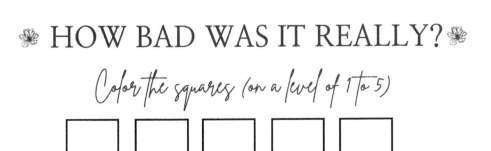

Daily PLANNER

Date _____

"Relax! Life is beautiful!"
David L. Wolper

WATER TRACKER
Fill in a drop for each glass you drink

ANXIETY CHECK
Rate your anxiety level (tick the circle)

○ Not anxious

○ A little anxious

○ Somewhat anxious

○ Pretty anxious

Thoughts

_____

_____

_____

_____

_____

_____

_____

Journal PROMPTS

❀ What three things make you the most anxious? ❀

❀ If I didn't experience anxiety, I wouldn't have learned this: ❀

What could you do right now that will make you really
❀ happy? ❀

Preparation TECHNIQUE

What's the situation?

What might make me feel anxious?

What can I say/ do to be prepared?

How have I handled it before?

Coping skills I can use

Grounding EXERCISE

Acknowledge 5 things you can touch 🌸

○ ○ ○ ○ ○

Acknowledge 4 things you can see 🌸

○ ○ ○ ○

Name 3 things you are grateful for 🌸

○ ○ ○

Acknowledge 2 things you can hear 🌸

○ ○

(Write it down in the circles)

Anxiety TRACKER

🌸 TRIGGER   REACTION 🌸

🌸 BETTER RESPONSE 🌸

🌸 HOW BAD WAS IT REALLY? 🌸

Color the squares (on a level of 1 to 5)

☐ ☐ ☐ ☐ ☐

Daily PLANNER

Date _____

"Almost everything you do will seem insignificant, but it is important that you do it"
Mahatma Gandhi

WATER TRACKER
Fill in a drop for each glass you drink

ANXIETY CHECK
Rate your anxiety level (tick the circle)

○ Not anxious

○ A little anxious

○ Somewhat anxious

○ Pretty anxious

Thoughts

_____

_____

_____

_____

_____

_____

_____

Journal PROMPTS

❀ What three things make you the most anxious? ❀

❀ If I didn't experience anxiety, I wouldn't have learned this: ❀

What could you do right now that will make you really
❀ happy? ❀

Preparation TECHNIQUE

What's the situation?

What might make me feel anxious?

What can I say/ do to be prepared?

How have I handled it before?

Coping skills I can use

Grounding EXERCISE

❀ Acknowledge 5 things you can touch ❀

◯ ◯ ◯ ◯ ◯

❀ Acknowledge 4 things you can see ❀

◯ ◯ ◯ ◯

❀ Name 3 things you are grateful for ❀

◯ ◯ ◯

❀ Acknowledge 2 things you can hear ❀

◯ ◯

(Write it down in the circles)

Anxiety TRACKER

❀ TRIGGER   REACTION ❀

❀ BETTER RESPONSE ❀

❀ HOW BAD WAS IT REALLY? ❀

Color the squares (on a level of 1 to 5)

☐ ☐ ☐ ☐ ☐

Daily PLANNER

Date _____

"Protect your enthusiasm from the negativity of others"
H. Jackson Brown, Jr.

WATER TRACKER
Fill in a drop for each glass you drink

ANXIETY CHECK
Rate your anxiety level (tick the circle)

◯ Not anxious

◯ A little anxious

◯ Somewhat anxious

◯ Pretty anxious

Thoughts

_____

_____

_____

_____

_____

_____

_____

Journal PROMPTS

❀ What three things make you the most anxious? ❀

❀ If I didn't experience anxiety, I wouldn't have learned this: ❀

What could you do right now that will make you really
❀ happy? ❀

Preparation TECHNIQUE

What's the situation?

What might make me feel anxious?

What can I say/ do to be prepared?

How have I handled it before?

Coping skills I can use

Grounding EXERCISE

❀ Acknowledge 5 things you can touch ❀

◯ ◯ ◯ ◯ ◯

❀ Acknowledge 4 things you can see ❀

◯ ◯ ◯ ◯

❀ Name 3 things you are grateful for ❀

◯ ◯ ◯

❀ Acknowledge 2 things you can hear ❀

◯ ◯

(Write it down in the circles)

Anxiety TRACKER

🌸 TRIGGER   REACTION 🌸

🌸 BETTER RESPONSE 🌸

🌸 HOW BAD WAS IT REALLY? 🌸

Color the squares (on a level of 1 to 5)

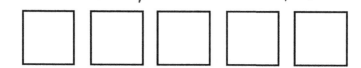

Daily PLANNER

Date _____

"Stay healthy, eat right and most importantly, be kind to all"
Tho Nguyen

WATER TRACKER
Fill in a drop for each glass you drink

ANXIETY CHECK
Rate your anxiety level (tick the circle)

○ Not anxious

○ A little anxious

○ Somewhat anxious

○ Pretty anxious

Thoughts

_____

_____

_____

_____

_____

_____

_____

_____

Journal PROMPTS

✤ What three things make you the most anxious? ✤

✤ If I didn't experience anxiety, I wouldn't have learned this: ✤

What could you do right now that will make you really
✤ happy? ✤

Preparation TECHNIQUE

What's the situation?   What might make me feel anxious?

What can I say/ do to be prepared?   How have I handled it before?

Coping skills I can use

Grounding EXERCISE

🌸 Acknowledge 5 things you can touch 🌸

○ ○ ○ ○ ○

🌸 Acknowledge 4 things you can see 🌸

○ ○ ○ ○

🌸 Name 3 things you are grateful for 🌸

○ ○ ○

🌸 Acknowledge 2 things you can hear 🌸

○ ○

(Write it down in the circles)

Anxiety TRACKER

❀ TRIGGER   REACTION ❀

❀ BETTER RESPONSE ❀

❀ HOW BAD WAS IT REALLY? ❀

Color the squares (on a level of 1 to 5)

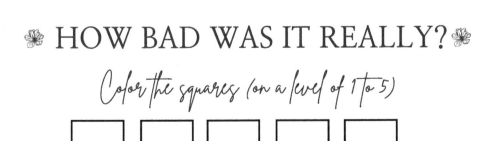

Daily PLANNER

Date _____

"A warm smile is the universal language of kindness"
William Arthur Ward

WATER TRACKER
Fill in a drop for each glass you drink

ANXIETY CHECK
Rate your anxiety level (tick the circle)

◯ Not anxious

◯ A little anxious

◯ Somewhat anxious

◯ Pretty anxious

Thoughts

_____

_____

_____

_____

_____

_____

_____

Journal PROMPTS

❀ What three things make you the most anxious? ❀

❀ If I didn't experience anxiety, I wouldn't have learned this: ❀

What could you do right now that will make you really ❀ happy? ❀

Preparation TECHNIQUE

What's the situation?

What might make me feel anxious?

What can I say/ do to be prepared?

How have I handled it before?

Coping skills I can use

Grounding EXERCISE

❀ Acknowledge 5 things you can touch ❀

◯ ◯ ◯ ◯ ◯

❀ Acknowledge 4 things you can see ❀

◯ ◯ ◯ ◯

❀ Name 3 things you are grateful for ❀

◯ ◯ ◯

❀ Acknowledge 2 things you can hear ❀

◯ ◯

(Write it down in the circles)

Made in United States
North Haven, CT
25 April 2023

35875470R00068